With love
from

_____

to

_____

LITTLE ☆ STARS™

PISCES

A parent's guide to the little star of the family

JOHN ASTROP

with illustrations by the author

E L E M E N T

Shaftesbury, Dorset ● Rockport, Massachusetts
Brisbane, Queensland

© John Astrop 1994

Published in Great Britain in 1994 by
Element Books Ltd.
Longmead, Shaftesbury, Dorset

Published in the USA in 1994 by
Element, Inc.
42 Broadway, Rockport, MA 01966

Published in Australia in 1994 by
Element Books Ltd.
for Jacaranda Wiley Ltd.
33 Park Road, Milton, Brisbane, 4064

Printed and bound in Great Britain by
BPC Paulton Books Ltd.

British Library Cataloguing in Publication
data available

Library of Congress Cataloguing in publication
data available

ISBN 1-85230-548-7

CONTENTS

THE TWELVE SIGNS

Everyone knows a little about the twelve sun signs. It's the easiest way to approach real astrology without going to the trouble of casting up a chart for the exact time of birth. You won't learn everything about a person with the sun sign but you'll know a lot more than if you just use observation and guesswork. The sun is in roughly the same sign and degree of the zodiac at the same time every year. It's a nice astronomical event that doesn't need calculating. So if you're born between

May 22 and June 21 you'll be pretty sure you're a Gemini; between June 22 and July 23 then you're a Cancer and so on. Many people say how can you divide the human race into twelve sections and are there only twelve different types. Well for a start most people make assessments and judgements on their fellow humans with far smaller groups than that. Rich and poor, educated and non-educated, town girl, country boy, etc. Even with these very simple pigeon holes we can combine to make 'Rich educated town boy' and 'poor non-educated country girl'. We try to get as much information as we can about the others that we make relationships with through life. Astrology as a way of describing and understanding others is unsurpassed. Take the traditional meaning of the twelve signs:

Aries - is self-assertive, brave, energetic and pioneering.

Taurus - is careful, possessive, values material things, is able to build and make things grow.

Gemini - is bright-minded, curious, communicative and versatile.

Cancer - is sensitive, family orientated, protective and caring.

Leo - is creative, dramatic, a leader, showy and generous.

Virgo - is organised, critical, perfectionist and practical.

Libra - is balanced, diplomatic, harmonious, sociable, and likes beautiful things.

Scorpio - is strong-willed, magnetic, powerful, extreme, determined and recuperative.

Sagittarius - is adventurous, philosophical, far-thinking, blunt, truth-seeking.

Capricorn - is cautious, responsible, patient, persistent and ambitious.

Aquarius - is rebellious, unorthodox, humanitarian, idealistic, a fighter of good causes.

Pisces - is sensitive, imaginative, caring, visionary and sacrificing.

If you can find anyone in your circle of friends and acquaintances who isn't described pretty neatly by one of the above it would be surprising. Put the twelve signs into different lives and occupations and you see how it works. A Taurean priest would be more likely to devote his life to looking after the physical and material needs of his church members, feeding the poor, setting up charities. A Virgoan bank robber would plan meticulously and never commit spontaneous crimes. A Leo teacher would make learning an entertainment and a pleasure for her pupils.

So with parents and children. A Capricorn child handles the business of growing up and learning in a very different way to a Libran child. A Scorpio parent manages the family quite differently to an Aquarian. The old boast, 'I'm very fair, I treat all my children the same', may not be the best way to help your little ones at all. Our individual drive is the key to making a success of life. The time when we need the most acceptance of the way we are is in childhood. As a parent it's good to know the ways in which our little ones are like us but we must never forget the ways in which they are different.

LITTLE PISCES

Lights!...Cameras!...*Midsummer Night's Dream,* take one...enter stage front little Pisces riding a moonbeam...roll'em. Yes, the big tough old world of reality has faded for you and your family; you've just gained the script for a fantasy movie, a sonnet, a fashion collection and a pop song that went to number one. That's what little Pisceans do! Their world is the beautiful one they create in their minds and if we're lucky they share it with us. Your little Pisces will have all the charm in the world, impressionable, sensitive and highly creative. The ability to visualise every thought makes for the most delicious sense of fantasy, often with the little Fish not knowing the difference between the latter and reality. Confusing for others around but even more confusing for them. Some Pisceans spend the whole of their lives in this bemused reality/fantasy mix-up and manage to create beautiful songs, poems and movies out of it. Always in touch with where public taste is going next, even the ordinary, everyday Piscean

(are there any?) can pick the song that's going to be top of the hit parade or the garment that will be worn by everyone a year later. Highly emotional, they weep constantly, not only for their own hurts but also for everybody else's. In the

early years you can find your little Waterbabe crying just because she heard another little one cry down the street. So sensitive are they that, chameleon-like, they take on the qualities of those that they are with, even imitating voices and accents not out of mockery but out of sympathy. They learn quickly from this ability for mimicry and fit in well wherever they go, rarely being out of place in any environment. Hulking great lads or dainty little girls, there is something about a Pisces that brings out the protective instinct in everyone, but all of this highly sensitive and vulnerable-seeming stuff does not add up to weakness, far from it. The resilience of Pisces is somewhat like water which can in time wear away the hardest rock or, if coming up against an immovable object, will find a new route around and surround it. It's a powerful element and so are these little dreamers. They are spontaneous in their needs and actions, caring little for timetables and rulebooks. Whatever little Pisces tells you, take it with a pinch of sea-salt, never take it literally; they're not lies, it's just that everything to them is a creative opportunity to enhance and make more beautiful the boring, dreary facts. Sometimes the tough old world of reality may seem too much for them but the real thing that they should be protected from is themselves. The softest touch in the zodiac, they are at the mercy of their own caring generosity, the magnet for every lame dog in the vicinity and giving their all for others. They'll need a little help to save some for themselves.

THE BABY

This is the babe to pamper and pet, snug in a little cocoon whether in your arms or in the crib. Little Pisces, if given the choice, would have liked to have stayed in that warm watery womb for eternity so, initially, the more that life in the brash old world outside resembles that, the better. This one may need a great deal of soothing to compensate

 when human contact is missing and it's rare for a little Piscean to get along without a dummy or some such thing to suck on. These small characters start to tune in to sounds around them, often responding with little echoes of their own, even tears coming when something sounded like a cry. They learn by mimicry and by playing the simplest teaching games, imitating

each other's sounds, you can advance this little one's abilities surprisingly well. The first words usually come pretty quickly but there's no need to worry if they don't. In time, your little one will delight you with every whimsical utterance so that's going to be worth waiting for. Watch your little Piscean's eyes when they're not following you around. They're miles away in a place you'll never know. Your small Sea-shrimp is making one of his earliest trips to a fantasy ocean on the other side of the universe that he'll return to throughout his life. Years later his teacher will say, 'Come back to us Thomas, you're dreaming again' and she'll be right but why do teachers never realise it would be more fun if we could all go there!

THE FIRST THREE YEARS

Little Pisceans quickly develop the art of tuning in to everyone around them and are moved by not only their feelings but those of others. You will find your timetable being subtly shifted backwards and forwards almost without you realising how that happened. Pisces like to eat, sleep and drink when and where they feel like it. The fact that you discover that they, more often than not, feel hungry when it's time to sleep, will want breakfast at suppertime and so on, won't get you any better at making this a routine than the original one because they'll change it next week. You'll discover about this time that the Fish's food 'likes' come from another planet – chicken soup with pineapple juice, tomato sandwiches with jelly – ugh! These little tiddlers will hang awkwardly around your knees when other people's toddlers are hoofing it around in search of wild adventure and something moderately antisocial. Resist the temptation to shove your little one away saying 'don't be so silly, go and play with Miranda' or you'll find your little fish will turn into a permanent limpet. Cuddles and reassurance will have to be provided when and where necessary or you'll make a bigger problem for yourself. With more emotions and feelings than other signs, it takes a lot of getting used to for  one so tiny. Be patient, it all comes right in the end. The mundane stuff like potty training will be a series of successes and absent-minded failures until things finally settle down. There will be obstinate moments but as with most things you can get a small Pisces to do almost anything as long as you play-act it, sing it or joke it. These little characters bring out your creativity if not their own.

THE KINDERGARTEN

You may find, in the first days, that getting little Pisces to let go of your hand and go into a nursery school at all will be like trying to release the hold of a small octopus. You'll get further by creating some good fantasy promises of the magical toys and paintings he can do there, or maybe one of his imaginary friends (he has plenty of these) is there waiting for him. Settled at long last, you'll find the little Fish will happily find a group of small friends to look after. This is when you'll discover that every day he will arrive home a new, quite different character. Little Pisces mimics all

and sundry and that goes for bad behaviour as well as good. Don't run straight off to the doctor if your little one develops an alarming twitch or has started speaking out of the side of his mouth. Look first at the rest of the kids and you'll find his best friend little Georgie has a nervous twitch and Emma talks just a little bit out of the side of her mouth.

SCHOOL AND ONWARDS

The stories and the creative aspects of school life will be loved by little Pisces. The social life will be loved even more. Quick and sensitive response to little friends will make them popular in class and, although they rarely push themselves to the fore, they are always in demand for their inventiveness and sheer entertaining good company. Usually attracted more to the artistic subjects and less to the more practical ones they can sometimes surprise

even themselves. My little Piscean son at six or seven was a whizz at mental arithmetic, sending himself off to sleep at night by doubling numbers in his head 2,4,8,16,32 and so on. I suppose I shouldn't be surprised as Albert Einstein was a little Pisces. During this time the idealising aspect of your little dreamer will start to show. Small and big Pisceans put their loved ones and dearest friends on pedestals and are inconsolable when they are let down. This will happen interminably in the school years as friends fail to come up to the high ideals of your little dreamer. The school work will be coped with, sometimes even quite admirably, but will always take second place to the relationships.

THE THREE DIFFERENT
TYPES OF PISCES

THE DECANATES

Astrology traditionally divides each of the signs into three equal parts of ten degrees called the decanates. These give a slightly different quality to the sign depending on whether the child is born in the first, second or third ten days of the thirty-day period when one is in a sign. Each third is ruled by one of the three signs in the same element. Pisces is a Water sign and the three Water signs are Pisces, Cancer and Scorpio. The nature of Water signs is basically emotional so the following three types each has a different way of expressing their feeling natures.

First Decanate - February 20 to February 29

This is the part of Pisces that is most typical of the sign qualities. Pisces is a dreamer. This part of the sign produces the kind of person that is extremely sensitive to the thoughts and the feelings of others around them. In many ways this sympathy and feeling for others can make them easily seduced into becoming and doing what 'they' want. The other side of the coin however is the pop-star, fashion-leader, ad-man that knows just how to tap and exploit the mass feelings of the moment. Most Pisceans from this decanate have a little of each quality in them. One thing is certain, they are one of the most fluently imaginative people in the zodiac and if they find an outlet for their talents they can become very popular and successful. It seems, though, that no matter how successful they become, they still find a strong need to give, look after, and sacrifice for others. Many achieving great wealth devote themselves to charitable causes for

the rest of their lives. Elizabeth Taylor's work for
Aids victims is a good example.

Second Decanate - March 1 to March 10

This is the Practical Dreamer. This part of the
sign shares with Pisces the influence of the sign
of Cancer and the Moon. These Pisceans have a
supersensitive emotional nature that acts like a
psychic sponge, soaking up the feelings and
thoughts of others. In fact, the way they feel will
respond very strongly to the vibes that they pick
up from those around. They are able to tap into
popular taste, the hopes and desires of the masses
and can be very successful in exploiting this ability. Feelings, for them, are often related strongly
to the unconscious and to past experience.

Whether they experiment with psychic abilities or not, there will undoubtedly be a great potential for development in this area. They often have a deep underlying shyness contrasting with a great sensitivity and ability to make contact with other people. There are usually powerful links with the family or family traditions throughout life. Often a family occupation is carried on or a family business is inherited.

Third Decanate - March 11 to March 20

This is the Persuasive Dreamer, where Pisces is combined with the influences of Scorpio and the powerful planet Pluto. There is a strong entrepreneurial quality about the Pisceans from this part of the sign. They are able to see talents and possibilities in others and show them how they can develop successfully. They are also great propagandists for their own causes, often having quite magnetic personalities that attract devoted followers. There can be much crusading work with this decanate but mainly it will take the form of behind-the-scenes giving. These Pisceans have more energy than is usual with this sign and can work indefatigably at projects that are considered a worthy enough challenge. More adventurous and given to extremes than most of the other dreamers, they are represented by people such as David Livingstone the great explorer and missionary and Sir Malcolm Campbell who set his speed records in the 1920s on the flat sands at Daytona Beach, Florida.

OTHER LITTLE PISCES

Mums and Dads like you delighted in bringing up the following little dreamers. Yours will probably turn out to be even more famous!

First Decanate Pisces

Copernicus, George Washington, Frédéric Chopin, Victor Hugo, Enrico Caruso, Rudolf Steiner, Auguste Renoir, Andrés Segovia, John Steinbeck, Prince Andrew, Sidney Poitier, Johnny Cash, Sam Peckinpah, Elizabeth Taylor, Anthony Burgess, Lawrence Durrell, Nina Simone.

Second Decanate Pisces

Antonio Vivaldi, Cyrano de Bergerac, David Niven, Alexander Graham Bell, Maurice Ravel, Samuel Barber, Mickey Spillane, Colonel Yuri Gagarin, Harry Belafonte, Bert Bacharach, Dame Kiri Te Kanawa, Eddy Grant, Tom Wolfe, Jon Bon Jovi, Gloria Estefan, Bobby Fischer, Jean Harlow.

Third Decanate Pisces

David Livingstone, Sergei Diaghilev, Henrik Ibsen, Benjamino Gigli, Vaslav Nijinski, Albert Einstein, Liza Minnelli, Rudolf Nureyev, Jimmy Lee Swaggart, Michael Caine, Billy Crystal, Harold Wilson, Max Wall, Harry James, Jerry Lewis, Ursula Andress, Sir Malcolm Campbell, Johann Strauss.

AND NOW THE
PARENTS

THE ARIES PARENT

The good news!

The generous, powerful, success-orientated Aries parent may find the Pisces child an enchanting but confusing puzzle. Pisceans are sentimental, intuitive, tearful, compassionate, and responsive to every mood and feeling of everyone about them (that includes dogs, cats, goldfish and stuffed teddies). Aries will appreciate Junior's highly-coloured imaginative abilities and endeavour to bring these to concrete results. Both signs are creative and can bring quite different qualities to a shared project.

Pisces adds vivid im-
agination and Aries the
ability to make ideas a
reality. Aries's motives
may well have been to
defeat the challenge
and succeed while little
Pisces will have done
everything for the

pleasure of working with someone they love. The
Piscean basic drive is rarely personal achievement
and it is in giving rather than receiving that they
are most fulfilled. The deep feelings and sensitivity
of the little Fish, if allowed full range of expression, will find strength and confidence to help
others creatively. Aries are their own person, finding their individuality and independence and then
sticking to it come what may. The little Pisces are
made of more malleable stuff and will blend and
mould their character depending on who they are

with. Usually less secure than this powerful parent and idealising their loved ones, little Pisceans could lose all confidence without a great deal of praise and encouragement. The real uniting factor in this relationship of very different characters is affection. This is something that you both have a strong need to express and plenty of hugs and cuddles will go a long way in smoothing most difficulties that may occur.

...and now the bad news!

You operate on such different levels that there are bound to be a few misunderstandings. Aries's natural admiration of personal strength and achievement may miss the point and see Piscean sensitivity as weakness. All attempts to bulldoze the Fish into becoming super-heroic will result in Junior doing a disappearing act into the world of escapist fantasy. Pisceans, after receiving undue pressure in their early lives, can hide in their fantasies all their lives, becoming less and less in touch with reality and achieving nothing. This could waste the true Piscean caring talents which are as capable of achieving worldly success as Aries. Pisces feature prominently in medicine, nursing, painting, writing, film, music and fashion.

THE TAURUS PARENT

The good news!

Your home is full of the comforts and love that all sensitive children need. Your attitude to your children is as a gardener tending patiently all the material needs of the small seedlings to give them the best possible chance to develop into strong and healthy flowers. Little Pisces is a rare little plant, an orchid that may need very special attention to achieve the most perfect blossom. The down-to-earth but caring Taurean parent will find the enchanting little Piscean a delightful enigma.

Intuitive, rich in imagination and sensitivity, these small dreamers fluctuate between the worlds of fantasy and reality as if they were one. The Taurean parent will soon come to realise that only in encouraging the confident expression of these talents can young Pisces achieve a good foothold in the material world. Love of the great outdoors is something that you can share, you needing to feel the good earth beneath your feet and your small Pisces drinking in the freedom. A little barefoot running through the grass wouldn't hurt either of

you! Little Fish are the most vulnerable and yet potentially the most talented children of the twelve signs. Pisceans have an extreme impressionability that enables them to quickly tune in and respond to the needs and feelings of others. Even with unsympathetic bulldozing they can just as sensitively adapt and selflessly become what is demanded of them. Sadly, though, when the latter occurs they sacrifice their own needs and desires to such an extent that they cannot function well without another's opinion, becoming indecisive and unfulfilled. The Taurean love of beauty, harmony and tangible results can provide invaluable support in developing this unique identity and individuality, and is probably the best area where you can help little Pisces find true confidence.

...and now the bad news!

If rules are too strict or system and routine too

firmly geared to clockwatching, you may find little Pisces becoming devious and inventing stories to avoid doing things. Much of the time these stories will be so convincing that you will be totally fooled. However, truthfulness can become a contentious matter with the two of you. For you, a lie is a lie and you'll feel obliged to make a firm stand. For little Pisces, whose vivid imagination makes it difficult to separate their inventions from reality, there has to be a much broader interpretation.

THE GEMINI PARENT

The good news!

Ever since you were a child you have been able to mix fantasy with fact, elaborate convincingly on the smallest snippet of information in order to make a good story and generally become a fund of information for all and sundry. Gentle little Pisceans seem as elusive as the elves and sprites in the stories they'll love their Gemini parents to read to them. It should be obvious to a bright-minded Gemini like you to see how you make contact with these soft, sensitive dreamers. In one word, imagination. Geminis are blessed with more than a fair share of this useful commodity and love nothing more than to share it with others. Little Pisces's love for the world of fantasy will soon show in early play. Imaginary 'friends', daydreaming, and being ''lost to the world' are typical pastimes. Highly intuitive, and deeply sensitive, this little one may need more sympathetic encouragement than most to put firm feet on the ground. You will be quick to realise that sharing this child's imaginings and giving them concrete expression in creative outlets is the way to build confidence. All of this 'meeting of the minds' stuff, however, will

be enriched considerably with the addition of your love of social life. You like to have plenty of visitors yourself and encouraging your little Fish to do the same can be fulfilling. Though in some ways impractical, the small Piscean is almost psychically 'in touch' with the needs and feelings of others. Quick to sympathise and selflessly offer real help to any lame duck, hurt friend and tired parent, they can positively sparkle with efficiency.

...and now the bad news!

Although you share the ability to visualise things easily, you operate on different speed levels. You are quick-thinking, one thought leading to another, fast. Your little dreamer plays with an idea, lingering and almost living it out in real time, to the extent that sometimes you will think you've lost contact altogether. Occasional impatience giving way to outbursts of the sharp, critical Gemini tongue may well cause much more hurt than intended. Piscean feelings run deeper than you'll ever know and words that you will throw off with only a second thought cut deeply into this super-sensitive little sprat. A flick of the silvery tail and the resulting escape into 'never-never' land may leave you without a key to the door and a long wait until you are offered it again.

THE CANCER PARENT

The good news!

The protective Crab and the sensitive Fish belong in the same element, the deep watery world of emotions and feelings. You two make the strongest of connections without even saying a word. Each senses the other's needs and responds whilst the rest of the family, if they are more down-to-earth signs, are blissfully unaware. Underwater radar carries long distances and a Cancerian Mom knows when her little Piscean falls down at school. Little Pisces picks up Crabby old Dad's 'bad days at the office' and comforts him without being asked. You will share a love of imaginative, creative ideas and activity. Cancer will always be sensitive to young Pisces's need to express in physical ways the rich sense of fantasy and highly inventive imagination this child possesses. Cancer will understand that the young Piscean comes to terms with the reality of life through the realisation of ideas rather than through accumulating facts and figures. Pisceans are sensitive to the needs and desires of others, and adapt easily to

each new demand. This natural ease at falling in with what others want may, however, become so comfortable for family relations that the Cancer parent fails to notice that Junior's individual needs are not being met. Never pushy in stating their own wants and believing, like themselves, that others in the family should know unasked what is needed, they tend to lose out every time. Unfulfilled ideas and individuality in the Piscean child are thrown inwards and reflect in daydreaming and fantasising. Sharing and appreciating these abilities will develop a gentle giant of confident creativity.

...and now the bad news!

The gentleness of this colourful little Fish brings out the strongest protective instincts in Cancer. Stepping in and helping out when things look tough sounds like good parental care but may not be so beneficial if taken to excess in this relationship. Little Pisces is always so amenable that if you want to do everything for him he'll be generous and let you. You'll make a rod for your own back and leave Junior ill-equipped for the big launch into the outside world. He'll never turn into a nasty spoilt monster, Pisceans always have too much charm, but someone else, later on, will have to pick up this big helpless Jellyfish and get him standing on his own two feet!

THE LEO PARENT

The good news!

Leos have a natural sense of family pride that
requires the best of recognition for their children,
wanting them to shine like the rays of Leo's rul-
ing planet, the sun. Although gentle little Pisces
doesn't yearn for a name in lights, preferring to
take a back seat, this child can be just cause for
Leo pride. Gifted with vivid imagination, often with
artistic and musical ability and, not least, a compassionate sympathy for all living creatures, young
Pisces can certainly make this loving parent's

breast swell. However, unlike the Lion, a young Pisces doesn't crave the applause. True, both signs share a love of play acting, but whereas Leo is up there for the cheers, Pisces enjoys the sheer delight of make-believe. Nevertheless, sharing this world of fantasy can build a close, loving relationship with oceans of fun. Big-hearted Leo, understanding the value of praise, can boost the sometimes fragile Piscean confidence, giving Junior a firm foot in the world of reality. Given security, the great imaginative powers of this child can often develop into an exceptional talent. Leos

themselves need to be appreciated and even admired so much that they find it easy to dish out large helpings of the same to their little charges, giving encouragement and confidence at the time it's most needed. Always! Positively, because little Pisces admires and seeks to emulate your great creative energy, this relationship can produce a more go ahead, and if not more practical, more effective, way of expression than one would usually expect.

...and now the bad news!

Most Pisceans in response to encouragement show creative talents; however, Leo's ambitions are lofty, and pushing your child into the spotlight prematurely, though possible is rarely desirable. Little Pisces, with loving devotion and a desire to please, may try hard to fit the bill, but the strain of this uncharacteristic role may prove too much. You will stand centre stage for the fame and acclaim whether it be in social life or in work while little Pisces's drive is just to react and sensitively respond to those around them. In your own enthusiasm you may not notice that you're losing something of your little one's own ability. Let little Pisceans shine with their own light and not yours.

THE VIRGO PARENT

The good news!

Like all opposite signs of the zodiac Virgo and Pisces have the basic ingredients for a good balanced relationship; with open minds each has much to learn from the other. Virgo's practical, down-to-earth realism contrasts widely with little Pisces' highly imaginative, impressionable and almost mystical idealism. For the little Fishes the borderline between vivid imagination and reality is undefined and it will take patient and sensitive guidance to separate the two. Junior's daydreaming, far from being useless for practical day-to-day living, can, if given full expression, become a positive talent and source of tangible achievement. Virgo's routine approach can be enhanced by sharing this youngster's world of fantasy, and by giving encouragement to write, draw, and act out these imaginings so as to develop little Pisces's self-confidence. Both parent and child share a love of caring for others though the way in which this manifests itself with these two quite opposite characters may not seem like it to each other. Many Virgo's answer to any and every problem is to tidy

up everything in sight, believing that others feel like themselves that most problems occur because people are in such a mess. Little Pisces on the other hand wouldn't even notice if she was sitting in the middle of the utmost squalor if she felt happy and believes that it's only what you feel inside that counts. Little Pisces for this reason may not help around the house as much as desired, but if the parent is ill or tired, the sensitive and caring side of Junior's sympathetic nature comes out and all the help in the world will be available. Looking after pets is a good way to combine a practical outlet for all this caring, feeling nature.

...and now the bad news!

There will inevitably be times when the daydreaming aspect of little Pisces will just seem like out and out laziness and work just has to be done. Constant nagging rarely get results with the little

Fish and usually succeeds in producing evasive tactics. Thrown into the negative use of all that imagination little Pisceans can come up with more convincing excuses than you can find jobs! They can lie and believe it and the more you provoke this talent the more it develops. Always finding it hard to tell the difference between the truth and reality, you'll have unwittingly set up a path of no return. Boring old chores will get done if you create some imaginative and fantasy outcome.

THE LIBRA PARENT

The good news!

Your basic nature is easy-going and sociable with an ability to relate to others in a balanced and cooperative way. There are not going to be any rigid hard and fast rules in your home and although you're never disorganised you prefer to play things as and when they're needed. You have just the brand of friendliness that can bring dreamy little Pisces out of the land of make-believe and into the world of reality. Without a bump! Vulnerable little Pisceans have a wealth of intuition and imagination that enables them to live utopian dreams inside their heads when the going gets tough. When they are 'far away' you can bet that they're in a better place than we are. The Libra parent, however, can encourage this small Fish to confidently express and share these talents with all. Fairness at all costs is an important factor for you and plenty of good conversation and friendly discussion will be one of your greatest shared pleasures. Both of you love the artistic and the beautiful and would benefit from regular sessions of shared creativity – painting, writing and play-acting are all Piscean favourites. With you being such a great team-worker and little Pisces responding so well to

closeness you'll both gain immense pleasure. You may well get some worthy results too. As your little Fish grows you'll get more help around the house if you've set up this working relationship earlier. Always consult your Junior partner on matters of colour, materials and decoration – amongst the wild ideas there may be a few unthought of possibilities.

...and now the bad news!

Parent and child have a sympathetic and sensitive approach in relating to others that precludes any real disagreement. In fact it would be difficult to say whether parent or child would be most horrified in the unlikely event of a battle. Smoothly as this team will run, little Pisces will quickly become overdependent if the Libra parent adapts too willingly to every whim. Not hugely ambitious, little Pisces will be only too pleased to take all the waiting on that you care to give. Unless you want a lazy old Jellyfish, share the fantasy and fun but encourage self-reliance in allowing Junior to do things for you. Through helping others little Pisceans find their real vocation in this world.

♏

THE SCORPIO PARENT

The good news!

Passion in the broadest sense rules your life. What you care about, you are devoted to. In order to achieve that which you desire you are prepared to spend phenomenal energy. You have a strong sensitivity to the thoughts and feelings of other people and an intense desire to do what is best for your children. With this sensitive child you have someone to share your deep feeling nature and awareness. This can be one of the most loving and sensitive relationships in the book. For many children the powerful Scorpio is admirably strong but a little daunting to try and live up to. Not so for little Pisces, who can deal with your great passion; having such deep feelings themselves, they can really understand you more than any other sign in the zodiac. Scorpio parents, intense and devoted, can be positive entrepreneurs where their children are concerned, gently guiding and encouraging their particular talents to fulfilment. The intuitive and highly imaginative little Pisces has much to offer in the way of artistic ability, and an almost psychic awareness gives this child a sympathetic insight into other people's

thoughts and feelings. The extraordinary vividness of Junior's imagination will be loved and allowed full expression by the admiring Scorpio parent. By coaxing these fantasies out of the head and into drawings, stories, and little acted-out scenes, Junior can be encouraged to distinguish the borderline between make-believe and reality. As long as Scorpio's support remains unobtrusive, the little Piscean poet can build real self-confidence with this powerful parent.

...and now the bad news!

You will defend your young ones to the last, but sensing Pisces's extreme vulnerability, you may be tempted to go to extremes. Over-protectiveness will guarantee a clinging vine, with Pisces readily escaping into daydreams and letting you get on with it when the going gets tough. These youngsters are not so soft as they sometimes behave.

They have a resilience that can often bounce back where others break. Remember the old story of the solid tree that snaps in the strong wind when the slender reed gives and returns unharmed and upright when the storm is over. That's your little Fishy. The yielding quality has real meaning when you realise that these youngsters need to give and it is in helping others that they find real fulfilment. If Junior can help you in really practical ways, self-assurance and efficiency will positively grow.

The Sagittarius Parent

The good news!

The important things that you value are honesty, straightforwardness and freedom. You believe in these things not only for yourself but for others also. You are energetic and outgoing and approach parenthood with a good sporty sense of fun and adventure. In fact if life is a journey you're one of the best fellow travellers if the kids can keep up with you. The warm, active, extrovert Sagittarian parent can be a perfect balance to the warm, loving, introvert little Piscean. These two contrasting characters, one outward-looking and the other inward-looking, have much to teach each other. They share a love of travel both mentally and physically, and this may provide one of this couple's closest links. Adventure stories about far away places will appeal to both and are good bedtime reading. Getting out and about and running free in the countryside is yet another great mutual pleasure. Little Pisceans have exceptional imaginative and intuitive talents that often make it difficult to define the borderline between make-believe and

reality. Sagittarius's philosophical nature and long-term vision will see the potential and encourage the physical expression of the small Fish's ideas. The 'if you feel it say it' attitude will go an enormous way towards developing self-confidence and, above all, a supremely trusting relationship. Never forget that this impressionable and undemanding child will adapt easily to any role the parent suggests in a desire to please. If the role is amenable and pleasant it may never be noticed that little Pisces's needs are not really being met.

...and now the bad news!

Little Pisces can tell fibs without even thinking. The borderline between fantasy and reality is blurred in this imaginative child's head. Sagittarians hate lies and can dish out truth themselves like a blunt instrument. This can hurt little Pisces more than you'll ever know. Often the little Fish's intention is less to deceive than to soften the harsh reality of just that kind of reaction. If this gets into a catch twenty-two situation where little Pisces inventively 'improves' the truth in case you're cross and you're cross because..... This may need a back to the beginning approach and plenty of reassuring cuddles before you can set things aright.

THE CAPRICORN PARENT

The good news!

You care what other people think and go to great lengths to earn the respect of those around you. This goes especially for your family for whom you are ambitious and caring. You give a great deal of hard work to providing for your loved ones and ask only in return that a child should be well-mannered, obedient and dutiful and should generally prove to be a credit to the family. Unlike many other signs, the Piscean child complies almost too easily with this parent's demands. Little Pisceans are pliable – they lend themselves readily to suggestions and will attempt to fit the mould their guardians have prepared for them. Though comfortable for the parent this may be less helpful to the child, whose impressionable young personality can easily be swamped by an upbringing that is too rigid, too defined. Although Pisces children will often go to the limits to live up to their parent's expectations, basically little Fishes resent restriction. They are gifted with a glorious imagination which needs plenty of freedom of expression to achieve real, practical results. Although the practical nature of Capricorn, if sensitive to

young Pisces's abilities, can be invaluable in helping to bring intangible ideas into reality, don't lose
the really far out quality of little Pisces's imaginings
in favour of more sensible ideas. The best in creativity is never just 'sensible'! Encouragement to
express their own intuitions and feelings in storytelling, creative projects and views on everyday
things will contribute greatly to the development
of Piscean self-confidence. When contact with this
other-world dreamer is lost, and from time to time
it will be, you can bring him back to earth with
some good Capricorn humour.

...and now the bad news!

Much of what you hold dear will be quite in-
comprehensible to little Pisces. The world of
reality has not the great attraction for one with
so infinite an imagination. You will find it hard
not to reprimand the constant flights of fancy and

daydreaming instead of getting down to what they should be doing. Too much emphasis on the no-nonsense mundane world will get the opposite result to the one you would like. Little Pisces will retreat more and more into her made-up world and pay only lip service to your demands.

THE AQUARIUS PARENT

The good news!

Aquarian parents are often universal aunts or uncles; never displaying favouritism, their affection is distributed equally between all children in their care. This includes nephews, nieces, friends' offspring, waifs and strays alike. In their eyes every living creature deserves an equal share of love. Little Pisces, however, needs a slightly more equal share than most. Your love of fairness to all and sundry keeps you a little on the detached side, believing that a good chat can solve almost anything. Not so with your little dreamer. Super-sensitive, highly imaginative, small Fishes give everything when they love someone and so require an extra large measure of affection in return and this means demonstrative love. A hug and a cuddle will do more good in this relationship than all the cajoling words you can muster. Both parent and child are idealists but the expression of this differs. Aquarians take a logical, reasoned approach to try and change things for the better; with little

Pisces the vision and fantasy take over and idealise those for whom he or she cares. Caring for others can be a shared meeting point. Little Pisces will respond well to any cause that you believe in and, if allowed to join in, will enthusiastically help save the environment, support wildlife preservation, collect for the underprivileged or just enjoy looking after the family pet. This parent's love of the new, unusual and the unexpected will relate well to the unlimited imagination of the little Piscean. Encouragement to express ideas inventively in music, dance, writing, and painting may uncover a wealth of talent, and will certainly develop independence – and self-assurance.

...and now the bad news!

You live your life on a mental level with logic, a good intellect and a need to understand everything. Little Pisces's motivation is emotional and feelings guide all actions. Help is needed to be able to express these feelings with ease but as little Pisceans are usually so amenable and cooperative their need may be missed altogether. If lacking confidence and finding no outlet for deep emotions, small Fishes will retreat into their other world. The Piscean vision is better shared than thrown inwards – better another poet for the world than a dropout dreamer.

THE PISCES PARENT

The good news!

One thing is certain, you are one of the most imaginative people in the zodiac and if you can find an outlet for your talent for daydreaming then you're made for life. It seems that no matter how successful you become in making your own way in life, you'll find a strong need to give, look after and sacrifice for others. Your moment has arrived for you now have somebody that wants to do the same for you. This is one of the most mutually loving parent/child relationships; the Piscean need to care for others is often taken to the point of self-sacrifice but with a little reciprocal attention you can relax the altruistic tendencies a little. Pisces Senior will understand the dreamy nature of highly imaginative little Pisces, sharing and developing the creative potential that is so strong in this sign. Finding a way in which Junior's talents can be developed will be a top priority. Always with a Piscean try the arts first, writing, painting and above all music and dance. Little girl Fishes dream of being ballerinas and some make it. Little boys too, for

both Nureyev and Nijinsky and even Sergei Diaghilev, the ballet impresario, were Pisceans. At least see if the reality is possible before settling just for the dream. With such an inventive mind Junior can live more easily in the rosy world of make-believe when the reality of living gets tough. Plenty of encouragement to express these thoughts through easy conversations, storytelling, and imaginative games will result in exceptional self-expressive abilities. Though often thought to be impractical, little Pisceans, like their parents, give of their best and show great efficiency when helping others. Through being allowed to assist Mum and Dad as often as possible, confidence in handling the 'nuts and bolts' side of life will grow.

...and now the bad news!

The biggest snag in this otherwise perfect relationship is not in clashes or argument but in excessive 'giving in', each wishing to please the other. Taken to extremes this natural Piscean quality can leave Junior with no real awareness of self. The Piscean dreams are better out than in, as the world can't afford to lose another creative idealist or artist. Having a greater understanding of your own sign, you are the one parent that can afford to be a little stronger in pushing little Pisces's real needs to the fore.

ON THE CUSP

Many people whose children are born on the day the sun changes signs are not sure whether they come under one sign or another. Some say one is supposed to be a little bit of each but this is rarely true. Adjoining signs are very different to each other so checking up can make everything clear. The opposite table gives the exact Greenwich Mean Time (GMT) when the sun moves into Pisces and when it leaves. Subtract or add the hours indicated below for your nearest big city.

AMSTERDAM	GMT + 01.00	MADRID	GMT + 01.00
ATHENS	GMT + 02.00	MELBOURNE	GMT + 10.00
BOMBAY	GMT + 05.30	MONTREAL	GMT - 05.00
CAIRO	GMT + 02.00	NEW YORK	GMT - 05.00
CALGARY	GMT - 07.00	PARIS	GMT + 01.00
CHICAGO	GMT - 06.00	ROME	GMT + 01.00
DURBAN	GMT + 02.00	S.FRANCISCO	GMT - 08.00
GIBRALTAR	GMT + 01.00	SYDNEY	GMT + 10.00
HOUSTON	GMT - 06.00	TOKYO	GMT + 09.00
LONDON	GMT 00.00	WELLINGTON	GMT + 12.00

DATE	ENTERS PISCES	GMT	LEAVES PISCES	GMT
1984	FEB 19	11.16 AM	MAR 20	10.24 AM
1985	FEB 18	5.08 PM	MAR 20	4.14 PM
1986	FEB 18	10.58 PM	MAR 20	10.03 PM
1987	FEB 19	4.50 AM	MAR 21	3.52 AM
1988	FEB 19	10.35 AM	MAR 20	9.39 AM
1989	FEB 18	4.21 PM	MAR 20	3.28 PM
1990	FEB 18	10.14 PM	MAR 20	9.19 PM
1991	FEB 19	3.59 AM	MAR 21	3.02 AM
1992	FEB 19	9.44 AM	MAR 20	8.48 AM
1993	FEB 18	3.35 PM	MAR 20	2.41 PM
1994	FEB 18	9.22 PM	MAR 20	8.28 PM
1995	FEB 19	3.11 AM	MAR 21	2.14 AM
1996	FEB 19	9.01 AM	MAR 20	8.03 AM
1997	FEB 18	2.52 PM	MAR 20	1.55 PM
1998	FEB 18	8.55 PM	MAR 20	7.55 PM
1999	FEB 19	2.47 AM	MAR 21	1.46 AM
2000	FEB 19	8.34 AM	MAR 20	7.35 AM
2001	FEB 18	2.28 PM	MAR 20	1.31 PM
2002	FEB 18	8.14 PM	MAR 20	7.17 PM
2003	FEB 19	2.01 AM	MAR 21	12.59 AM
2004	FEB 19	7.51 AM	MAR 20	6.49 AM

John Astrop is an astrologer and author, has written and illustrated over two hundred books for children, is a little Scorpio married to a little Cancerian artist, has one little Capricorn psychologist, one little Pisces songwriter, one little Virgo traveller and a little Aries rock guitarist. The cats are little Sagittarians.